KNOW
THE FACTS

KNOW THE FACTS ABOUT
DRINKING AND SMOKING

Paul Mason

rosen publishing's
rosen
central®

New York

Published in 2010 by The Rosen Publishing Group Inc.
29 East 21st Street, New York, NY 10010

Copyright © 2010 Wayland/The Rosen Publishing Group, Inc.

First Edition

Series editor: Nicola Edwards
Consultant: David Ferguson
Designer: Rawshock Design
Picture researcher: Kathy Lockley
Artwork by Ian Thompson

Library of Congress Cataloging-in-Publication Data

Mason, Paul, 1967–
 Know the facts about drinking and smoking / Paul Mason. – 1st ed.
     p. cm. – (Know the facts)
 Includes index.
  ISBN 978-1-4358-5339-3 (library binding)
  ISBN 978-1-4358-5462-8 (paperback)
  ISBN 978-1-4358-5463-5 (6-pack)
  1. Drinking of alcoholic beverages–Juvenile literature. 2. Smoking–
Juvenile literature. 3. Youth–Alcohol use–Juvenile literature.
4. Youth–Tobacco use–Juvenile literature. I. Title.
HV5066.M265 2010
613.81–dc22

2008053162

Picture Acknowledgements:
All pictures of young people posed by models. The author and publisher would like to thank the models, and the
following for allowing their pictures to be reproduced in this publication: Jean Pierre Amet /Corbis: 41; Bill
Bachman/Alamy: 30; Bettmann/Corbis: 4; John Birdsall/Alamy: 6; CNRI/Science Photo Library: 19; © Daimler
Chrysler: 25; Randy Faris/Corbis: 13; David Hoffman Photo Library/Alamy: 20; image100/Corbis: 16, 32; Lucas
Jackson/Reuters/Corbis: 42; Michael A. Keller/zefa/Corbis:7; Frank Kletschkus/Alamy: 39; Matthias
Kulka/zefa/Corbis: 28; Kuttig-People/Alamy: 21; Chris McLennan/Alamy: 35; Photodisc/Alamy: 33; PHOTOTAKE
Inc/Alamy: 22; Erin Ryan/zefa/Corbis: 26; Sam Scott-Hunter/Photofusion Photo Library: 36; SGO/Image Point
FR/Corbis: 31; Stephen Shepherd/Alamy: 37; Adrian Sherratt/Alamy: 45; Simon de Trey-White/Photofusion
Photo Library: 15; Visions of America, LLC/Alamy: 5; Janine Wiedel/Photofusion Photo Library: 27; Peter
M.Wilson/Corbis: 38

Grateful thanks to Andrew Fusek Peters and Polly Peters for their permission to use the poem *Fag Off* on
page 23.

Manufactured in China

CONTENTS

Polluting the body   4
Smoking: a growth industry   6
Alcohol: the world's favorite drug   8
Smoking and the human body   10
Alcohol and the human body   12
Binge drinking   16
Long-term effects   18
Addiction   26
Pressure to drink and smoke   32
The cost to society   36
Is there a "safe" level?   40
Drinking, smoking, and the law   42
Tomorrow's health today   44
Glossary   46
Further information and Web Sites   47
Index   48

POLLUTING THE BODY

Imagine you're growing some award-winning cabbages. They don't need much help: just water, sunshine, and clean air. Now imagine giving your cabbages polluted water and dirty air. No awards for them now! They smell funny, and don't grow properly. People who drink alcohol and smoke cigarettes are doing the same thing—but to their bodies, instead of their cabbages.

Legal drugs

Alcoholic drinks and cigarettes both contain drugs that have a short-term effect on the human body. Humans have used alcohol and nicotine (the drug in tobacco) for thousands of years, because those short-term effects feel pleasant. Unfortunately, we now know that drinking and smoking also have medium- and long-term effects that are very **UN**pleasant. Both drugs are linked to terrible diseases and premature death.

Doctors now know that alcohol and tobacco are more dangerous to people's health than some drugs that are banned. But alcohol and tobacco have been around for a long time and are very popular—so popular that governments would probably find it impossible to ban them outright. When the U.S. government tried to stop people drinking alcohol between 1920 and 1933, the attempt failed completely: people simply continued drinking illegally. Attempts by other governments to ban alcohol have proved so unpopular that they had to be repealed, or canceled.

Alcohol was banned in the United States between 1920 and 1933, during a period which was called Prohibition. Here, Prohibition agents are destroying stocks of illegal alcohol. Other governments have also tried to ban alcohol, including Russia (1914–25), Iceland (1915–22), Norway (1916–27), Hungary (1919), and Finland (1919–32).

Big-bucks industries

Today, drinking and smoking are the basis for businesses that earn billions of dollars every year. Tobacco growers, cigarette manufacturers, wine makers, distilleries, and breweries make the raw materials. Bars, restaurants, liquor stores, supermarkets, and other retailers sell these products. They all pay tax to governments —sometimes huge amounts of tax. In China, for example, in the year 2000, 9.05 percent of the government's tax income came from cigarette tax.

Smoking is common in China, where over a third of people smoke. The Chinese government earns almost a tenth of its tax income from taxes on cigarettes.

SPEAK YOUR MIND

"I like smoking—I think it makes me look cool."

"My mom's been a smoker since she was 16. She says it's made her look old—her skin's much more wrinkly than someone's who doesn't smoke."

"I drink with my friends—I enjoy getting drunk, it's fun."

SMOKING: A GROWTH INDUSTRY

Ever since pre-rolled cigarettes were first introduced in the early 1900s, the number of cigarettes smoked around the world has risen each year. Today, over 15 billion cigarettes are smoked EVERY DAY. Even though the number of cigarettes smoked in some countries is falling, overall consumption continues to go up. There are two main reasons for this:

• **Selling more cigarettes in poorer countries**

Tobacco companies know that there is a huge potential market for their cigarettes in poorer countries. In wealthy countries, such as the U.S.A., the U.K., France, and Australia, 1,500–2,500 manufactured cigarettes per year are sold for every member of the population. In contrast, in countries such as Peru, Zambia, Ethiopia, India, and Bangladesh, fewer than 500 cigarettes per person are sold.

In China, as the country has become wealthier, the number of manufactured cigarettes smoked has leapt from 1 per man per day in 1952, to 15 in 1996. If people in poorer countries follow the same path, the number of smokers in the world will grow massively.

• **Expanding world population**

The world's population is forecast to increase from 6 billion to at least 8 billion by 2030. Even if the proportion of smokers falls, the actual number of smokers will probably grow.

An ad for cigarettes in India. There are about 120 million smokers in India, and smoking is estimated to be responsible for 900,000 deaths in the country each year.

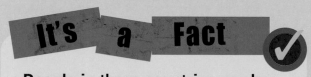

It's a Fact ✓

People in these countries smoke the most cigarettes each year:

China	(1,643 billion cigarettes)
U.S.A.	(451 billion)
Japan	(328 billion)
Russia	(258 billion)
Indonesia	(215 billion)

Smoking rates among young people are highest in Eastern Europe, India, and some islands in the Western Pacific. Around the world, 40 percent of children are exposed to passive smoking at home when they breathe in the smoke from someone else's cigarette.

Who smokes more and who smokes less

Whether people smoke depends a lot on their sex, age, level of education, and where they live. Smoking is on the increase in the world's poorer countries. Smoking is becoming less popular in wealthy countries, especially among men. Among women, smoking is declining in the U.S.A., Canada, Australia, and the U.K., for example, but not in southern Europe or Japan. Smoking among young people is increasing among girls, but not among boys.

WHAT'S THE PROBLEM?

"I like eating takeouts and sweets, but I don't want to get fat. My friend told me that if you smoke, it makes you thinner. Is that right?"

No, it isn't. Smoking doesn't stop your body absorbing nutrients from food: if you eat fast food all the time, you'll get fat, whether you smoke or not. If you eat healthily and exercise regularly, you won't get fat.

ALCOHOL: THE WORLD'S FAVORITE DRUG

Our favorite drug is alcohol. The World Health Organization estimated in 2004 that at least 2 billion people around the world drank alcohol. The amount people drink increased from just under 8.5 pints (4 liters) of pure alcohol for each person over the age of 15 in 1961, to 12.7 pints (6 liters) in 1981. By the end of the 1980s, the figure had fallen to just over 10.5 pints (5 liters) a year, and has stayed steady at this level ever since.

Who drinks, how much, and where

As with smoking, the amount people drink is linked to where they live, how wealthy they are, their religion, and whether they are male or female:

• **Location**

People drink the most in Europe and the Americas. Europeans are by far the biggest drinkers. In the early 1980s, when the amount people were drinking in these regions peaked, Europeans were each drinking 36 pints (17 liters) a year compared to 17 pints (8 liters) in the Americas. Even by 2000, it was about 21 pints (10 liters) against 12.7 pints (6 liters).

The amount children from wealthy countries drink has increased enormously in the last 30 years.

• Wealth

Given a choice between buying food for a week or alcoholic drinks, most people choose to eat. When the choice is between alcohol and the latest movie on DVD, more people opt to buy a drink. This is the basic reason why drinking alcohol is closely linked to wealth, and especially to disposable income (the amount of spare money people have).

• Europeans have the highest disposable incomes, and drink the most.
• North Americans have a higher disposable income, and South Americans a much lower one; overall, they drink less alcohol than Europeans.
• The two regions where alcohol consumption has risen in recent years—Western Pacific and Southeast Asia—are places that have also seen rises in disposable income.

• Religion

Religion has an important effect on alcoholic consumption, because Muslims are forbidden by their religion to drink alcohol. Muslim countries such as Kuwait, Libya, Saudi Arabia, and Bangladesh, for example, do not record any alcohol being drunk by their citizens.

• Sex

In general, women drink less than men, and more women than men avoid alcohol entirely. In the U.S.A., for example, 29.3 percent of men and 38.2 percent of women abstain from drinking. Men are also more likely to be heavy drinkers than women, although this is changing. In the U.K., for example, 39 percent of male drinkers are heavy drinkers—but female heavy drinkers, who now tip the bar at 42 percent, have recently overtaken them.

The 10 biggest consumers of alcohol are:
1 Uganda*
2 Luxemburg
3 Czech Republic
4 Ireland
5 Republic of Moldova
6 France
7 Reunion
8 Bermuda
9 Germany
10 Croatia

----
*based on estimated consumption of home-brewed alcohol.

SMOKING AND THE HUMAN BODY

What happens to the body when a smoker lights up a cigarette?
As soon as a smoker lights up, the tobacco smoke is drawn into the lungs. The smoke is made up of several ingredients: not only the drug nicotine, but also tar particles, a poisonous gas called carbon monoxide, and other chemicals.

From cigarette to brain

Within seconds of the first puff, the active ingredients of the cigarette are in the smoker's bloodstream and whirling around the body toward the brain.

When they reach the brain, the ingredients imitate chemicals called endorphins and dopamines, which occur naturally in the body and are associated with pleasure. Nicotine is a relatively weak drug, so it produces only temporary feelings of slight pleasure.

In many countries, smoking in workplaces has been banned because of the dangerous effects of passive smoking. Smokers now have to stand outside in all weathers to get their fix.

Other effects

While a cigarette's active ingredients are stimulating the smoker's brain, other substances in the cigarette smoke are having different effects:

- Carbon monoxide is absorbed into the smoker's bloodstream, making it harder for the blood to carry oxygen around the body. Oxygen is essential for keeping the body working.
- Other toxic substances in the smoke are also absorbed into the bloodstream, where they begin to have a long-term effect on the smoker's body.
- The tar particles in cigarette smoke gather in the smoker's lungs, where they will form a tarry sludge. This stops the lungs from working properly, because part of their area is covered with tar and cannot absorb oxygen to pass on to the blood.

It's a Fact

Someone who smokes dramatically increases their chances of dying from a smoking-related disease. Professor Richard Peto, a cancer specialist, describes the risk in this way: "If you [take] 1,000 young adult smokers, one will be murdered, six will die on the roads, but 500 will die from tobacco."

Passive smoking

Passive smoking happens when people nearby breathe in the smoke from a cigarette. It has a similar effect on their body as it has on the smoker's, and means that even nonsmokers are affected by cigarette smoking.

WHAT'S THE PROBLEM?

"I asked my mom why she smoked and she said that smoking helps her to relax. She always goes outside to smoke, even in cold weather and rain. It doesn't look very relaxing to me. Is there anything I can say to change her mind?"

You could tell her that, rather than helping smokers to relax, smoking a cigarette actually increases the heart rate. Smokers feel at ease when they smoke, because they're given a short rest from their craving for nicotine. There are lots of ways to relax that don't involve cigarettes. Page 47 has a list of places to find ways of encouraging someone to give up cigarettes and helping them once they've made the decision to stop smoking.

ALCOHOL AND THE HUMAN BODY

People drink alcohol for lots of reasons—one of the main ones is because they like how it makes them feel. Like the nicotine in tobacco, alcohol has a physical effect on the human body. Many people feel that alcohol helps them to relax, and nicotine is often said to have the same effect.

Drinking an alcoholic drink is like going on a trip—a trip that can end in a number of places, depending on when you stop drinking.

Alcohol is measured in "standard drinks," each of which contains 0.6 ounces (13.7 grams) of pure alcohol. A 5-ounce glass of wine or a 12-ounce bottle of beer count as one drink. U.S. guidelines suggest that women should drink no more than 7 drinks, and men no more than 14, per week. There is no safe amount of alcohol for children, whose bodies and minds are still developing.

Stage 1—"Please board the aircraft"

This is the happy, first stage of the journey, traveling through relaxing scenery and looking forward to the trip. When you first have a drink, your body absorbs the alcohol very quickly. (How quickly depends mainly on how much you've eaten and what type of alcohol you drink.)

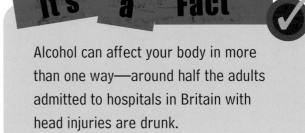

It's a Fact

Alcohol can affect your body in more than one way—around half the adults admitted to hospitals in Britain with head injuries are drunk.

Alcohol acts as a depressant. It depresses our fears and inhibitions, which is why many people feel happier when they first have a drink. It's also why lots of people feel more confident than normal after drinking alcohol.

Stage 2—"Fasten your seat belts: turbulence ahead"

Alcohol also affects the human body in other ways. These get more obvious the more you drink:

- Alcohol affects our coordination, making even simple tasks, such as walking or picking things up, harder than normal.
- People's reactions get slower and slower the more they drink.
- Speech becomes slurred and decision-making becomes increasingly difficult.

What Would you do? ❓

Your sister is a really nice girl, but when she goes out, she drinks loads and her personality seems to change: she starts dancing (even when there's no music) and she gets really loud and shouts at people. What can you do to help her? Do you:

a) Hide her purse so she won't have any money to buy drinks when she goes out.

b) When you next have a quiet time on your own with your sister, calmly explain to her how worried you are, and how embarrassing you find the way she behaves when she's drunk.

c) Video her dancing and shouting while she's drunk and show it to her later, hoping she'll be so ashamed that she'll never touch another drop.

Turn to page 47 for the answers.

On their journey with alcohol, these people are in the departure lounge: everyone is feeling relaxed and happy. If they keep drinking, though, there may be a bumpy ride ahead.

Stage 3—a bumpy ride

The human body doesn't really like alcohol. It automatically recognizes that alcohol stops the body from working properly, and that large amounts are generally deadly. To get rid of it, the body breaks down alcohol in the liver, then washes it out of the body in urine. Cleaning alcohol out of the bloodstream takes the human body quite a while—much longer than it takes to drink it. The result can be a vicious cycle:

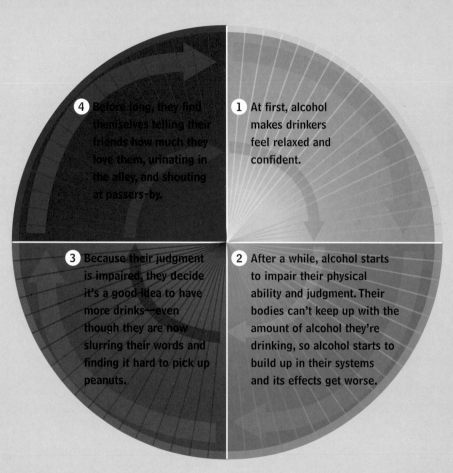

4 Before long, they find themselves telling their friends how much they love them, urinating in the alley, and shouting at passers-by.

1 At first, alcohol makes drinkers feel relaxed and confident.

3 Because their judgment is impaired, they decide it's a good idea to have more drinks—even though they are now slurring their words and finding it hard to pick up peanuts.

2 After a while, alcohol starts to impair their physical ability and judgment. Their bodies can't keep up with the amount of alcohol they're drinking, so alcohol starts to build up in their systems and its effects get worse.

Stage 4—a crash landing

The effects of drinking alcohol last long after a person stops drinking. As well as being a depressant, alcohol is a diuretic drug—which means that drinking it makes people want to urinate a lot. Over time, this causes the body to become dehydrated (lacking in water), which in turn causes headaches, tiredness, and a dry, sticky mouth. As well as this, while the liver is working to break down alcohol, it is too busy to supply energy to the brain (which is one of the liver's other jobs). This leads to mood swings, decreased concentration, and a reduced attention span.

It takes a blood alcohol content of about **0.25** percent to make a person sick. Anyone who keeps drinking after this is likely to be in real danger of dying.

It's a Fact ✓

The effects of alcohol change as it builds up in your bloodstream. The amount in your blood in called your Blood Alcohol Concentration (BAC):

EUPHORIA (BAC = 0.03 to 0.12%): good mood and confidence, but shorter attention span, poor judgment, and movement.

LETHARGY (BAC = 0.09 to 0.25%): feeling sleepy, difficulty understanding and remembering things, difficulty walking, blurry vision.

CONFUSION (BAC = 0.18 to 0.30%): feeling confused, dizziness, poor speech and vision, overemotional, and vomiting.

STUPOR (BAC = 0.25 to 0.40%): inability to move around, temporary or semipermanent loss of consciousness, death through choking on own vomit.

COMA (BAC = 0.35 to 0.50%): body begins to shut down, heart rate drops, coma or death becomes increasingly likely.

DEATH (BAC more than 0.50%): this level of alcohol causes the central nervous system to shut down and is likely to cause death.

BINGE DRINKING

Not everyone agrees on what binge drinking is, but today when people talk about it, they usually mean drinking a lot of alcohol over a short period of time. Binge drinkers often set out planning to get as drunk as possible as quickly as possible. Binge drinking is a growing problem, especially among young people.

The risks of binge drinking

Binge drinking is a dangerous activity. Quickly drinking a lot of alcohol effectively poisons your body, and regularly leads to drinkers dying. There are other dangers to binge drinking, too.

Binge drinking leaves girls unlikely to be able to make sensible decisions about whether they want to have sex or not, and less able to resist pressure to have sex.

- The poor decision-making that comes from drinking too much means that people don't recognize dangerous situations. They are more likely to be involved in a motor accident, or to be mugged or attacked in some other way.
- The aggression and overconfidence some people feel when they have drunk too much makes it more likely that they will get into a fight.

Social effects

Binge drinking causes problems for society as a whole, not only for the drinkers themselves. People who are very drunk lose their inhibitions and find it difficult to make good decisions. They also become overemotional and sometimes violent.

In the U.K., after pubs and clubs close in many city centers on the weekends, the streets fill with young people who have drunk too much alcohol. Fights and attacks often break out, and many police forces now have to have extra officers on duty to deal with the problem.

Binge drinking costs businesses huge amounts of money, mainly because their employees miss work with hangovers (there is more information about this on pages 32–33).

Walking home alone might not seem such a good idea if you were sober.

SPEAK YOUR MIND

"My friend got really drunk at a party, and ended up in a bedroom with a boy. She thinks they were just kissing, but she can't really remember what happened. Now he's saying that she slept with him, and the whole school is saying she's a slut."

"I go clubbing with my friends every Friday night. We get really wasted—it's great. I have to stay in bed most of Saturday, though, until my hangover goes away."

LONG-TERM EFFECTS

The effects of drinking and smoking aren't limited to the short and medium term. Over long periods of time, both can seriously affect your health. Alcohol- and smoking-related diseases mean that vast amounts of money are spent each year on caring for drinkers and smokers. Of course, this money could otherwise be spent on looking after the sick and dying, or trying to find cures for diseases.

Global effect of alcohol

According to the World Health Organization (WHO), about 2 billion people around the world drink alcohol. Of these, about 76.3 million have some kind of problems as a result: there are direct links between drinking alcohol and over 60 different types of disease and injury, including cancer of the throat, getting run over by a car (which is more likely to happen to you if you have been drinking), and committing or being the victim of a murder. By far the biggest risk for drinkers is the increased chance that they will develop some kind of disease because of the alcohol they drink.

Long-term health effects of drinking

Most people know that long-term alcohol abuse can cause diseases of the liver. It's the liver that cleans alcohol from your blood, so it does suffer especially badly in heavy drinkers. But long-term use of alcohol is linked to a long list of other health problems, including:

- cirrhosis and hepatitis (both diseases of the liver)
- gastritis (soreness and swelling of the stomach lining) or pancreatitis (soreness and swelling of the pancreas)

One of the health problems associated with heavy drinking is obesity. This man is sporting a generous "beer belly."

- high blood pressure (which can lead to stroke) and heart failure
- several types of cancer, including mouth and throat
- damage to the brain and problems such as epilepsy
- vitamin deficiency, muscle disease, and skin problems
- obesity
- sexual problems and infertility.

Long-term effects of binge drinking

Less is known about the long-term health effects of binge drinking, because it is a relatively new area of study. However, some evidence links binge drinking to early death, especially due to sudden heart attack.

WHAT'S THE PROBLEM?

"I'm worried about the amount my dad drinks. He goes to a bar most nights and he usually keeps on drinking when he gets home. He gets in a bad mood when he wants a drink, but he says you can't become an alcoholic if you only drink beer. Is that right?"

No, it isn't. Beer contains alcohol, just like wine, whiskey, vodka, and all the other drinks behind the bar. Your dad is putting his health at risk by the amount he drinks. You cannot make up his mind for him, but you can support him if he decides to cut down on his drinking. Turn to page 47 for a list of sources of help.

A healthy liver (left) next to an alcohol-damaged one (right).

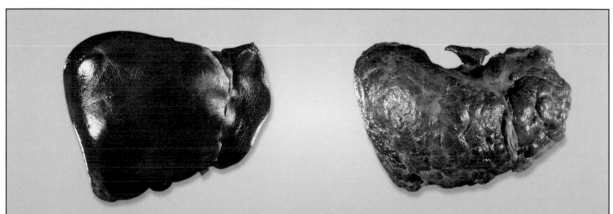

Alcohol, health, and young people

In the United States, the proportion of high school students who drink alcohol has fallen from 50 percent in 1999, to 45 percent in 2007. Also in 2007, about 26 percent of U.S. high school students reported binge drinking. But in the U.K., the amount that young people drink has risen dramatically. In fact, it has doubled, from three standard drinks a week in the early 1990s to 6 drinks a week in 2004. On top of this, by the time they are 13, more kids are drinking to excess than not. The immediate effects of this have been an increase in the number of young people killed in accidents or as a result of drinking too much.

In the U.K., every year over 1,000 children under the age of 15 are admitted to hospital emergency rooms suffering from alcohol poisoning.

It's a Fact

Some people argue that alcohol is less dangerous than drugs like marijuana, cocaine, or acid. In fact, alcohol is responsible for the deaths of more teenagers than any other drug.

The long-term effects of the increase in childhood drinking are not yet certain. But drinking has a cumulative effect: if you drink more, for longer, the health effects become worse. Starting young is likely to mean that health effects from alcohol appear sooner, and end up being worse.

Long-term effects of smoking

"Cigarettes," as the saying goes, "are killers that travel in packs." Smoking is linked to a wide variety of diseases, and in the U.S., it kills over 438,000 people a year. Some smoking-related health problems can be improved, or even gotten rid of entirely, by giving up. Others remain forever.

Most people start smoking young, while they are still at school. The health effects of smoking (including passive smoking) at a young age are especially severe. For

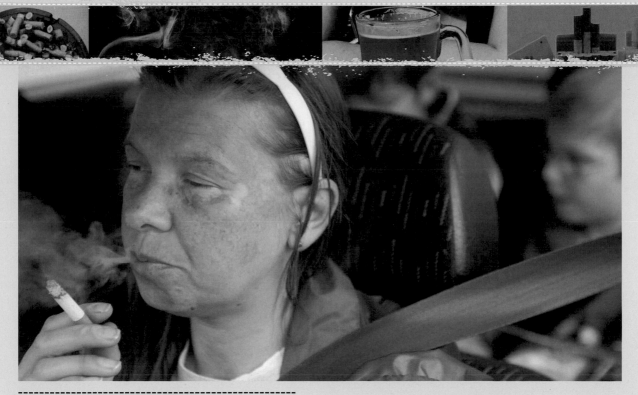

When people breathe in smoke from someone else's cigarette, both the smoke the cigarette releases as it sits in an ashtray and the smoke a smoker blows out are harmful to their health.

example, very young smokers are more likely to have breathing problems, such as sicknesses of the lungs and asthma. Their lungs will grow to be smaller and work less well, and they are likely to be shorter than their nonsmoking classmates. Passive smoking has been linked to sudden death in babies.

It's a Fact

Smoking is a lot more dangerous than crossing the street or driving: 24 times as many people are killed every year by smoking as die in road accidents.

What Would you do?

A couple of your friends at school have started smoking. They say you should try it too. You're not thrilled, but you don't want to look uncool. Do you:

a) Accept a cigarette, but try not to inhale the smoke?

b) Say you might start when you're older, but you can't afford cigarettes at the moment?

c) Tell them no thanks, you don't want your breath and your clothes to stink of smoke, and you don't want to risk dying of lung cancer?

Turn to page 47 for the answers.

Smoking-associated health problems

Smoking is so bad for you that every five minutes, a British smoker dies from a smoking-related disease. In the time it takes you to read this sentence, someone, somewhere in the world, will have died because they smoked.

• Lung problems

Smokers typically suffer from a variety of lung problems. They find it harder to breathe, and are more likely to get colds, flu, pneumonia, and asthma. Smoking is linked to a disease called emphysema; some emphysema sufferers have to carry breathing apparatus around with them. Smoking is also responsible for 90 percent of all lung cancers.

• Other cancers

As well as lung cancer, smoking is a major cause of cancers of the voice box, throat, esophagus, bladder, kidney, and pancreas.

• Other major health problems

It would be easy to fill several books with descriptions of all the bad health effects of smoking. Briefly, though, smoking is linked with many heart and circulatory problems, including brain damage because of strokes, heart attacks, and blindness. Poor circulation to the hands and feet as

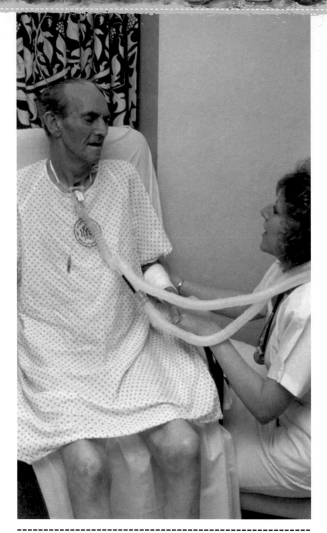

Each cigarette you smoke takes an average of 7 minutes off your life span. But it might be that living with the effects of smoking is as dreadful as dying from them.

a result of smoking can lead to them having to be amputated. Smoking is also connected with infertility, especially among men.

What's in a puff?

Here are a few of the nasty things in a typical puff of cigarette smoke (plus, other places you might find the same things):

- acetone (also found in paint stripper)
- ammonia (floor cleaner)
- arsenic (ant poison)
- butane (lighter fuel)
- carbon monoxide (exhaust fumes)
- DDT (an insecticide)

These are present only in tiny amounts—but if you smoke enough cigarettes, they can build up inside your body.

SPEAK YOUR MIND

"My grandma's been smoking since she was 15. Now she's got emphysema and she's in a really bad way. I hate seeing her suffer like that. I'm never going to smoke."

WHAT'S THE PROBLEM?

"My friend is pregnant and says she's going to continue smoking because she 'doesn't want a big baby.' But I'm worried she's going to damage the baby's health."

You are right to be worried. If your friend smokes while she is pregnant, she's more likely to have a small baby, and the baby is more likely to be born dead or with birth defects such as shrunken limbs. The baby will also grow up with increased nicotine receptors in its brain, making it more likely to become addicted to smoking when it grows up.

Your friend can get help to give up smoking—asking staff for advice at the hospital or doctor's office where she is going for her antenatal checks is a good place to start.

FAG OFF

When at school,
Fags were cool.
Not so young,
Removed right lung.
Hacking got to me,
Tracheotomy.
Ignore that boffin!
Carry on coffin'.
Finally led
To a boxed-in bed,
Nobody's fool,
I'm now dead cool.

- **From** Poems With Attitude **by Andrew Fusek Peters and Polly Peters (Wayland, 2000).**
NOTE: A "fag" is a British slang word for cigarette.

Cost

Health issues aside, there's another big problem for long-term drinkers and smokers—cost. In Britain, where cigarettes cost $10 a pack, average smokers spend enough on cigarettes to buy a brand-new car every three years if they gave up. For someone who becomes addicted to alcohol, the costs can be even higher. Some alcoholics can drink their way through $40 of alcohol a day—put another way, a new car every nine months or so.

The cost of smoking

The cost of smoking varies depending on where you live. Cigarettes are more expensive in some countries than others. It's always the case, though, that money spent on cigarettes could otherwise have been spent on food, clothing, transportation, or luxuries such as cars and vacations.

The cost of drinking

As with smoking, the average cost of drinking alcohol is different around the world, and depends on how much you drink. In the U.S., drinking at levels that are unsafe for your health will cost you at least $1,000.00 a year—and probably more than this.

It's a Fact ✓

Few people spend as much on cigarettes as the people of Minhang, in China, where the ashtrays must really be overflowing—smokers there spent on average 60 percent of their income on their habit.

Tax issues

One of the reasons that cigarettes and alcohol are expensive in many countries is that governments tax them heavily. They do this partly to try and discourage people from drinking and smoking too much. Some governments, as in the U.K. and other European countries, also raise money to pay for the treatment of alcohol- and smoking-related diseases.

Some people suggest that governments are too anxious to listen to alcohol and tobacco companies, because of the amount of money the industries provide in taxes. One example of this happened in 1997, when the British government delayed plans to ban tobacco advertising on Formula One race cars.

Heavy drinkers who quit would be able to buy the whole car, plus the engine of another one, in a year.

Average U.K. smokers could buy this much of the car in a year, if they gave up.

SPEAK YOUR MIND

"My mom gave up smoking last new year. She saves all the money she would have spent on cigarettes. This year, we're vacationing—and mom's paid for it with her savings!"

ADDICTION

The problem with "pleasure" drugs like alcohol and nicotine is that when we discover we like them, we want more and more. Our brains and bodies start to get used to having the drug coursing through our blood. If the drug is withdrawn for some reason, it feels uncomfortable— as though there is something missing. It becomes harder and harder to function properly without it. This is known as addiction.

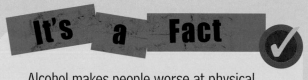
It's a Fact

Alcohol makes people worse at physical activity, not better. Unfortunately, it also increases confidence and lessens self-criticism, so someone who's drunk may THINK they're singing or playing the drums, or telling a joke better. People who have to listen to them may not agree…

Who becomes addicted?

What makes some people become addicts is complicated, and no one is sure of an exact answer. Experts do know that people react to drugs in different ways:

- A few people can use drugs such as nicotine or alcohol regularly for years, without becoming addicted or increasing the amount they take.
- Other people develop a very quick addiction to a drug, finding within just a few days that they cannot do without it.

- Many people develop an addiction over time. As their body gets used to dealing with the drug it is taking on board, more of the drug is needed to get the same effect. They steadily increase the amount they drink or smoke, for example. What was once an occasional cigarette or drink at a party becomes a 20-a-day habit, or the need to go out at lunchtime for a drink.

Alcohol addiction

Alcohol addiction is often called alcoholism. Most experts recognize alcoholism as a disease. Because alcohol affects people in different ways, health experts do not agree on an exact definition of alcoholism. One of the quick tests many doctors use to decide if a patient might be alcoholic is the CAGE test. The doctor asks the patient:

"Have you ever felt you needed to CUT down on your drinking?
"Have people ANNOYED you by criticizing your drinking?
"Have you ever felt GUILTY about drinking?
"Have you ever felt you needed a drink (known as an "EYE-OPENER") first thing in the morning?"

Two or more "yes" answers mean the patient may be alcoholic.

For some people, occasional drinking turns into a dangerous addiction called alcoholism, in which they are unable to function without regular intakes of alcohol.

Why do people become alcoholics?

Medical experts don't know for sure why some people become alcoholics and others don't. There are several factors that seem to show people who are more likely to become alcoholic than others:

- Living in an environment where there are lots of heavy drinkers, and where alcohol is regularly used.
- Extreme sadness or depression, for example, after the death of a child or loved one. Psychological illnesses are also associated with alcoholism.
- Some scientists think that a few people inherit genes that make them more likely to become alcoholic.

Nicotine addiction

The part of tobacco smoke to which people become physically addicted is the drug nicotine. Nicotine is a stimulant that affects the central nervous system. It works differently on different areas of the brain, which is why people can say that nicotine both "gets me going" and "relaxes me." People's bodies quickly get used to nicotine. As this happens, they have to smoke more and more to get the same effects. They are addicted.

Hooked

Smokers are hooked on their habit, like a fish on a line. If they try to wriggle off the hook by stopping smoking, their body starts to develop withdrawal symptoms, like these:

- a strong desire for tobacco
- a feeling of anxiety and difficulty sleeping
- bad temper, anger, and depression
- problems concentrating
- headaches, dizziness, and a feeling of tiredness

There are only two ways to get comfortable: start smoking again, or rough it for a few weeks and wait for the physical effects of the nicotine addiction to disappear.

People giving up smoking often suffer from constipation—sometimes they go for weeks without moving their bowels.

When a person inhales cigarette smoke, it takes seven seconds for the nicotine in it to reach the brain.

Social addiction

Cigarette and alcohol addiction are linked to people's lifestyles. For example, most people know a smoker who says things like: "I always have a cigarette with my coffee in the morning" or "I can't relax when I get home until I have a cigarette." Drinkers also often associate drinking with specific social events: going out on the weekend, meeting friends for Sunday brunch, getting home at the end of the day, and eating or finishing dinner, for example.

Stopping smoking or drinking is made harder by these associations. Not only do you have to deal with physical withdrawal symptoms, you also have to learn to break ingrained habits.

SPEAK YOUR MIND

"It's my body. I'm going to decide whether or not I smoke or drink alcohol."

"My uncle lost his job because his drinking was out of control. I think alcohol can be a very dangerous drug."

People can attend support groups to help them break free from their addiction to alcohol.

Recognizing addiction

The early stages of addiction, especially to alcohol, can be hard to detect. Many people drink at a low level, and even binge drinkers are not necessarily addicts. People in the early stages of alcohol addiction blend in with these other drinkers. It is sometimes takes years for their friends finally to realize that they are alcoholics.

WHAT'S THE PROBLEM?

"I first had an alcoholic drink a year ago. I've been drinking more and more, and now I'm worried that I'm addicted. How can I tell?"

The quick answer is that if you're asking, you probably do have a problem. Here are some questions to ask yourself:

- Have you ever promised yourself not to get drunk again, then gone out a few days later and done the same thing?
- Do you only go out to places that will serve alcohol?
- Do you find yourself having to drink more and more to feel drunk?
- Do you get shaky hands and become irritable if you don't have a drink?

If the answer to many of these questions is "yes," then you may be addicted to alcohol. Turn to page 47 for a list of sources of help.

Doctors have several treatments they can offer to people who want to give up smoking.

Addicted to cigarettes

The early stages of a smoking addiction are easier to detect. Very few people are able to smoke a cigarette or two once in a while, and stay at that level without smoking increasing numbers of cigarettes. In general, people who start smoking become addicted fairly quickly, even if they don't smoke every day. Once they are hooked, most people smoke increasingly frequently until they become a regular, heavy smoker.

It's a Fact

The longer people smoke, the harder they find it to stop. But even if someone only smokes for a short time, some of the harmful effects cannot be undone.

Dealing with addiction

If you are worried that you or someone you know has an alcohol or nicotine addiction, it is vital to get professional help. The best place to start looking for help is your family doctor. Alcoholics sometimes seek help from groups such as Alcoholics Anonymous, or at a residential facility.

If you are worried that a friend or someone in your family has an addiction, try to encourage them to visit the doctor and speak about it. Remember, though, that they have to recognize that they have a problem and want to deal with it—you cannot do it for them.

PRESSURE TO DRINK AND SMOKE

With all the evidence of how bad it is for you, it seems amazing that anyone ever starts drinking or smoking, let alone continues. And yet millions of people around the world continue to take up cigarettes and alcohol as though it will do them no harm at all. Why?

Peer pressure

Amazingly, many people don't especially want to start drinking or smoking. They do it—and sometimes keep doing it—because of pressure from their friends, or people they know. This is called peer pressure. Peer pressure works in different ways:

• Pressure from friends

A friend offers you a cigarette or a drink, and you don't want to say no. They're your friend, after all, and you don't want to quarrel with them.

• Pressure to fit in

A crowd of cool kids badger you into smoking, or you start doing it to impress them in the hope that they'll like you.

Whatever the pressure you feel, ask yourself if it's really a good idea to give in. It might feel like a good idea now. It probably won't years later, if you end up having to drag an oxygen canister around with you to help you breathe. See panel opposite and page 47 for more about resisting peer pressure.

Having to resist pressure from your peers to smoke or drink alcohol can make you feel uncomfortable. But standing up for what you believe in will increase your self confidence and self-esteem, and ultimately, other people's respect for you will increase, too.

It's a Fact

If you start smoking at the age of 15, you're three times more likely to die of cancer than if you start in your mid-20s.

WHAT'S THE PROBLEM?

"I was in the park with my friends last week and one of them brought out a bottle of vodka. My friend offered me a swig of it, and I said no—my grandfather was a heavy drinker and it killed him. But I'm worried that next time I'll be pressured into taking one."

This kind of pressure can be hard to resist, but people get used to the fact that you don't want to drink pretty quickly. It normally runs something like this:

• The "go on" stage: "Go on, have one. Tch—what's up? Why not? [*Insert possible abuse here.*] OK, suit yourself." This stage usually lasts for about two or three offers.

• The "X is a health freak/scared" stage: "[*Insert name here*] won't have one: they're too worried about getting liver disease at 97/caught by their mom," etc. This stage can last up to a month.

After this, you'll probably find that people will realize that you mean what you say and they'll stop pestering you. If someone's REALLY bullying you to start drinking alcohol—or smoking cigarettes—then, of course, they're not a friend at all.

Cigarette marketing

For years, cigarette manufacturers have been under threat from people concerned about the health effects of smoking. In wealthy countries, the health effects of smoking are widely known. Manufacturers have come up with several ways to keep their billion-dollar industry going:

- Promote "light" or "mild" cigarettes as a less-unhealthy alternative. In fact, these cigarettes carry similar health risks, and are far more dangerous than not smoking at all.
- Spend more on marketing. In the U.S., for example, $200 per smoker is spent every year on cigarette marketing.
- Increase efforts to sell cigarettes in poorer countries, where restrictions on advertising are less restrictive.

Indirect marketing

Tobacco and alcoholic beverage companies are experts at "indirect marketing." This basically means advertising in a way that has nothing to do with their products, or which you don't immediately notice. In 1993, a document from one tobacco company revealed how the company tried to influence public opinion: "We try to provide the media with statements in support of our positions from third-party sources, which carry more credibility... and have no apparent vested interest."

There are several different examples of indirect marketing:

• Sports sponsorship

By sponsoring sports teams and events, the companies hope that people will associate the glamor and healthy lifestyle of sports with their product. Of course, nothing could be less fitting: any benefits people get from exercise are largely wiped out if they regularly smoke or drink.

• Music and culture

In a similar way to sports events, the companies sponsor music concerts, art exhibitions, and a variety of other cultural events. Again, they hope that some of the glamor will rub off on their products.

• Movies and TV

Tobacco and drinks companies know that fans like to be like their heroes. If fans see a famous actor smoking a particular brand of cigarette, for example, maybe they'll start buying that brand, too.

Tobacco and booze fight back

The tobacco and alcoholic beverages companies don't like rules that might prevent them from making money. They spend vast amounts trying to persuade governments and others not to make it

Sponsoring sports teams is just one way for cigarette companies to advertise their products.

harder for them to sell cigarettes and alcohol. Between 1995 and 2000, for example, tobacco companies contributed more than $5 million to members of the U.S. Congress. If these Congressmen and women don't support the tobacco industry's point of view, they may later find it hard to secure additional contributions.

SPEAK YOUR MIND

"Seeing celebrities with cigarettes doesn't make me want to smoke—I don't want my skin to turn yellow and wrinkly, and I don't want to smell like an ashtray!"

THE COST TO SOCIETY

Both alcohol and nicotine abuse cost society dear, though not in exactly the same ways. Alcohol is linked to social problems such as crime and antisocial behavior. It also places tremendous strains on the healthcare system. Smoking's cost is mostly caused by the need to look after people who are suffering from smoking-related illnesses.

Alcohol and crime

Alcohol is closely linked with crime, which affects the whole of society. People who drink often feel more confident and aggressive: crimes such as muggings, burglaries, assaults, and murders are most likely to be committed by someone who has been drinking. Of course, the confidence that drinkers feel is misplaced, which is probably why so many drinking criminals get caught—over 60 percent of convicts in the U.K. admitted to drinking before they committed a crime.

Alcohol and antisocial behavior

Drinking is making some city centers in the U.K. no-go areas for ordinary people, who are scared of alcohol-related violence. A poll in 2003 found that binge drinking and antisocial behavior worried 78 percent of U.K. people. Partly as a result, only a quarter of people aged 35–54 went out in their city center more than once a week.

Violence in the U.K. often occurs in town centers at night, when large numbers of people have been drinking alcohol in bars and clubs.

Alcohol and health

In many countries, the health problems that result from alcohol abuse are getting worse. In Britain, for example, the number of people dying from alcohol-related cirrhosis of the liver increased by four times between 1971 and 2001. WHO suggests that alcohol is the third-biggest health risk in wealthy countries. Treating people—the sick, and those who have become addicted to alcohol but want to give it up—costs the health service billions every year.

Many people find the streets a scary place to be. Street drinkers, especially in groups, can be threatening and aggressive.

SPEAK YOUR MIND

"My brother was mugged for his cell phone in the street by someone who'd been drinking—he could smell the sour alcohol on his breath."

Smoking's social benefits?

The tobacco industry sometimes argues that smoking is good for the economy. It points out the huge amounts of tax governments earn from smokers, and the numbers of people who earn money through tobacco, from growers to people working in cigarette factories and those who sell cigarettes.

The tobacco industry has even claimed that early deaths through smoking have benefits for society as a whole. A 2001 report on the Czech Republic commissioned by Philip Morris, one of the world's biggest tobacco companies, said that Czech smokers lived 5.23 years less than nonsmokers. It suggested that:
"Public finance benefits from smoking… via savings on the health care costs, in pensions, and public housing costs savings."

In other words, if people are dead from smoking, they don't need doctors, money, or a place to live.

Economic costs

In fact, the smoking industry has high economic costs for society. The most important is the cost to the healthcare system. Treating the various diseases caused by smoking comes at a very high price. In 2002, the smoking costs of healthcare in various countries were:
- U.S. $76 billion
- Canada $1.6 billion
- U.K. $2.25 billion
- Germany $14.7 billion
- China $3.5 billion
- Australia $6 billion
- New Zealand $84 million

Smoking has other costs for society. These include:

This tobacco crop is being grown on farm land in Cuba.

• Land

Tobacco is grown on good farmland. In poorer countries especially, this land could instead be used to grow food for people who currently do not have enough.

• Fires

Every year, fires caused by careless smoking damage landscapes and buildings. In China in 1987, the world's worst forest fire killed at least 300 people and made 5,000 homeless. The fire had been started by a thrown-away cigarette.

• Environment

Thrown-away cigarette butts have environmental costs. In Australia, for example, there were estimated to be about 700,000 cigarette butts in the sand at Sydney's popular Bondi Beach. The butts take over 10 years to rot, and end up in the water, damaging wildlife, and making swimming unpleasant.

• Time off

The cost of people leaving the workplace for cigarette breaks or having days off sick for cigarette-related illnesses is tremendous. For example, in the U.S. in 2001, nonsmokers took an average of 3.86 days off sick; ex-smokers took 4.53 days; and smokers were off sick for 6.16 days.

In an attempt to cut smoking and littering, smoking is now banned on many Sydney beaches.

IS THERE A "SAFE" LEVEL?

People often have the idea that there is a "safe" level of alcohol or nicotine use, which won't do you any harm. Even if this were true, most people's use of alcohol and nicotine increases over time, so they would be unlikely to stay at a safe level. But is there a healthy amount that you can drink or smoke?

Alcohol

The effect of alcohol on your body is different depending on how old you are and how much you drink. Alcohol is most dangerous for the very young.

• Unborn children can be seriously affected if their mother drinks alcohol. A condition known as Fetal Alcohol Syndrome affects their physical, mental, and emotional development, and the effects last for life.

WHAT'S THE PROBLEM?

"My friend says that drinking doesn't do you any harm as long as you aren't getting drunk all the time. In fact, he says he's heard that it's good for you. Is he right about that?"

There is some evidence that older people, especially men, get slight cardiac health benefits from drinking one glass of red wine each day, and that elderly women gain slightly increased brain power if they drink a small amount. So if you're a middle-aged man or a female senior citizen, your friend is right.

SPEAK YOUR MIND

"Someone I know drinks in the park with her friends—some of them bring bottles that they've swiped from their parents. I used to think she was cool, until one night, she got so drunk she was sick everywhere, and then she passed out. She was a real mess."

- By the time children reach their teens, regular drinking makes it more likely that they will develop health problems, including alcoholism, in later life.
- By adulthood, many doctors say that drinking two drinks a day for men and one drink a day for women is unlikely to do any serious harm.

Smoking

Even moderate regular smoking carries similar health risks to heavy smoking. There is very little evidence of smoking being good for you, but some claims have been made. In particular, smoking is said to reduce the chances of developing Alzheimer's Disease and Parkinson's Disease. However, since you are more likely to develop health problems due to smoking than either of these diseases as a nonsmoker, only a very misguided person would take up smoking for the possible health "benefits."

Hospital treatment for smoking. When smokers are sick, they are more likely to be motivated to try to give up the habit.

"I can't see any more, my hands and feet are always cold, and I suffer from heart problems. One of my sons has problems with his lungs whenever the weather is cold, and the other one is a heavy smoker himself. And it's all because I used to smoke 40 cigarettes a day."

DRINKING, SMOKING, AND THE LAW

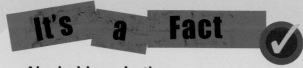
Alcohol laws in the United States

• Under 21

Alcoholic beverages may not be purchased by people who are under 21 years of age.

• Photo ID card

In most U.S. states, in order to purchase alcohol from a supermarket, liquor store, or other vendor—or to drink alcohol in a restaurant, bar, or other public venue—you must show a photograph ID card such as a driver's licence, a passport, or a state ID card that clearly shows from your date of birth that you are older than 21.

• Limited sales

In about 10 percent of U.S. counties, the sale of alcohol is prohibited either all or some of the time—these are called "dry" counties. Some states restrict the alcoholic content of drinks that may be sold, such as Utah, where beer cannot exceed 3.2 percent alcohol content. Also under Utah law, packaged alcoholic beverages can only be purchased from state-approved stores.

Governments now know how dangerous it is for people to drink and smoke, especially excessively. Because of this, they have introduced laws to stop people—in particular young people—from having access to alcohol and cigarettes.

In many places, drinking on the streets has been made illegal in an effort to stop antisocial behavior by drinkers.

What the law says—alcohol

In almost all countries, it is illegal for people under the age of 18 to buy or drink alcohol. A few countries have lower limits: in France and Belgium, for example, you can buy or drink alcohol at 15. Some set a higher limit: in the U.S., for example, you

Because of the health risks to people breathing in someone else's smoke, smoking in public indoors has been banned in some countries.

must be 21, and in Japan 20. A few countries have different rules for different types of alcohol: in Egypt, you can buy beer at 18, but must be 21 to buy anything else (though you must be 21 to drink any kind of alcohol).

What the law says—smoking

In many countries, buying or smoking cigarettes is illegal for under-18s. The authorities in the U.K., many U.S. and Australian states, New Zealand, and elsewhere have brought in bans on smoking in public enclosed spaces and workplaces.

It's a Fact

If you're a smoker, don't try and take a vacation in Bhutan: in 2004, it became illegal to buy cigarettes there. In 2006, smoking in public was made illegal, making Bhutan the first country in the world to ban smoking.

TOMORROW'S HEALTH TODAY

The choices you make about drinking and smoking when you are young will influence the rest of your life. If you become a heavy smoker or drinker, the chances are that it will make your life less pleasant, as well as shorter. Despite years of medical research supporting this fact, some people refuse to accept it:

• **"I can beat the odds"**
Some drinkers and smokers will swear blind that the statistics lie—drinking and smoking don't necessarily affect your health. And yes, everyone has heard a story about someone who had a great uncle who smoked 20 a day until he died at 103. But these great uncles (if they really exist at all) are extremely rare. Most smokers die younger than nonsmokers.

"Go on, just try one." He's almost sure to pay a heavy price if he does.

• **"I'll worry about it when I'm older. Who wants to live to be 60?"**
The simple answer is, most 59-year-olds do. Health warnings about smoking and drinking seem pretty irrelevant when you're young. "Trouble breathing when I'm 40? I'll probably be dead before then anyway! Pass me another cigarette!" "A heart attack at 45? Getting drunk tonight won't make any difference to that! Pour me another drink!" These are easy answers at 16—but they won't be very comforting when you're 39 or 44.

Living with the results of drinking and smoking

Discussions about drinking and smoking often focus on your life expectancy (how long you can expect to live). But dying may not be the worst result of developing a drinking or smoking habit. The worst thing may be living with the effects. Ask yourself a few questions:

• How would you like to have to trail an oxygen canister round behind you 24 hours a day in your 30s, like some smokers who develop emphysema?

A little exercise has lots of benefits: it gives you more energy, it makes you less likely to be sick, and it can even help you to do better at school.

- Would it suit you to have a leg amputated in your 40s, because of poor circulation due to smoking?
- How would you like to start seeing things, develop yellow skin, and begin vomiting blood as a result of drinking alcohol?

There are plenty of other dreadful effects of drinking and smoking—and if you develop a habit when you're young, you're much more likely to find out about them at first hand. It's up to you whether you drink or smoke—just check out the facts!

SPEAK YOUR MIND

"My husband and I really wanted to have children, but even though we tried and tried, it wouldn't happen. The doctors told us that smoking might be part of the reason."

Glossary

abstain completely stop doing something

active ingredients the ingredients in a mixture that have an effect

alcoholic person who is addicted to drinks that contain alcohol

alcoholism the condition of being an alcoholic

amputated cut off. In humans, amputations are usually of digits (fingers and toes) or limbs (arms and legs)

ban to forbid or make illegal

Blood Alcohol Concentration (BAC) the measure of the amount of alcohol in a person's blood

cardiac to do with the heart

cirrhosis disease of the liver, which results in healthy liver tissue being replaced by scar tissue. Since the liver is vital for survival, any damage of this kind is extremely dangerous

constipation inability to pass feces, i.e. not being able to have a bowel movement

cumulative building up or increasing. The effects of alcohol and cigarettes are cumulative: the more you drink or smoke, the worse they get

DDT short for DichloroDiphenylTrichloroethane, a toxic insecticide that was commonly used until the mid-1970s

dehydrated lacking water

depressant drug that temporarily slows down the body's functions

depression deep unhappiness, hopelessness, or both

disposable income the amount of spare money a person has

diuretic making someone urinate

genes units inside the human body that transmit characteristics like blond hair or brown eyes from one parent to child

hangover the unpleasant effects of drinking too much alcohol

heavy drinkers people who regularly drink so much alcohol that it has a physical effect on them

HIV short for Human Immunodeficiency Virus, a disease that destroys the body's ability to fight off disease

hypothermia dangerously low body temperature

imitate behave in a similar way

impair make something work less well

insecticide a chemical mixture designed to kill insects, stopping them from eating crops, or sometimes, spreading disease

marketing persuading people to buy

pancreas organ of the body that releases crucial chemicals, called hormones, into the bloodstream

passive smoking breathing in smoke from another person's cigarette

poll survey or questioning

premature earlier than expected

repealed undone or canceled, especially a law

sexually transmitted diseases diseases such as HIV, syphilis, or herpes that are passed on from one person to another during sex

stimulant drug that temporarily speeds up the body's functions

stroke injury caused when a blood vessels in the brain suddenly bursts

toxic poisonous

withdrawal symptoms painful or uncomfortable effects of stopping taking a drug

Further information

BOOKS

An Overview For Teens: Smoking
Margaret O Hyde (21st Century Books, 2005)

Drinking: A Love Story
Caroline Knapp (Dial Press Trade, 2007)

Dry: A Memoir
Augusten Burrows (Picador, 2004)

Making Smart Choices About Cigarettes, Drugs, And Alcohol
Sandra Giddens (Rosen Central, 2008)

The Easy Way to Stop Smoking
Allen Carr (Sterling, 2005)

WEB SITES

Due to the changing nature of Internet links, Rosen Publishing has developed an online list of Web sites related to the subject of this book. This site is regularly updated. Please use this link to access this list: www.rosenlinks.com/ktf/drin

WHAT WOULD YOU DO?

Page 13

Answer (a) will just make your sister angry—and she can always get her friends to buy drinks for her instead; answer (c) might work in the short term, but is unlikely to put her off getting drunk for long. Answer (b) is the best way go start getting your sister to think seriously about the amount she is drinking and the effect it is having—not just on her, but on others like yourself, too.

Page 21

Don't let your friends put pressure on you to take up smoking—they're more likely to respect you for confidently saying no rather than giving in to pressure. Answer (b) is risky, because they might just try to give you cigarettes to encourage you to join them. Answer (c) allows you to make the point that the effects of smoking are deeply uncool, both in the short and longer terms. If your friends won't accept your point of view, are they really such good friends?

INDEX

Numbers in bold refer to illustrations.

addiction 24, 25, 28, 30, 31
advertising 6, **6**, 24, 34, **35**
alcohol 4, 8, **8**, 9, 12, **12**, 13,
   13, 14, 15, 16, 18, 19, 20,
   24, 25, 26, 27, 30, 31, 32, 33,
   36, 37, **37**, 40, 42, 43
   ban on 4, **4**
   companies 25, 34
   cost of 24, 25, 37
   effects of 4, 12, 13, 14, 15,
     15, 18, 19, 20, 37, 40,
     44, 45
   poisoning 16, 20, **20**
alcoholism 27, **27**, 28, 40
Americas 8, 9
antisocial behavior 36, **36**,
   37, **42**
Australia 6, 39, **39**, 43

Bangladesh 6, 9
binge drinking 16, **16**, 17, 19,
   30, 36
blood alcohol concentration 15
bloodstream 10, 11, 14, 19
brain 10, 11, 14, 19, 26, 29

carbon monoxide 10, 11
China 6, 7, 25
cigarettes 4, **5**, 6, **6**, **7**, 10, **10**,
   11, 20, 21, **21**, **23**, 24, 27,
   31, 32, **32**, 33, 34, 35, 38, 42
craving 11
crime 36, 36, 37

dangerous situations 16, 21
death 4, 11, 15, 16, 19, 20, 21,
   23, 33, 37, 38

diseases 4, 11, 18, 20, 21, 22,
   24, 36, 37, 38, 39, 44
doctors 4, **31**, 40
dopamines 10
drugs 4, 10, 14, 20, 26, 27, 28
drunks 17, 26

endorphins 10
Europe 8, 9
exercise 7, **45**

food 7, 24
France 6, 9

governments 4, 5, 25, 34, 37,
   38, 42

hangovers 17

India 6, **6**
indirect marketing 34

Japan 7

Kuwait 9

laws 42, 43
Libya 9
liver 14, 19, **19**
lungs 11, 21, 22

men 9

nicotine 4, 10, 11, 12, 23, 26,
   28, 29, 31, 36, 40

obesity 18, **18**

passive smoking 10, 11, 20, 21,
   21

peer pressure 32, **32**, 33, **33**,
   44
Peru 6

religion 9
Russia 7

smoking 5, **5**, 6, 7, **7**, 8, **8**, 10,
   10, 11, 20, 21, 22, 23, 24,
   28, 29, 29, 31, 41, 44, **44**, 45
   ban on 39, **39**, 43, **43**
   cost of 24, 25, 36, 38, 39
   effects of 4, 10, 11, 18, 20,
     21, 22, **22**, 23, 34, 36,
     40, 44, 45
   giving up 11, 20, 23, 24,
     28, 31, **31**, 41
Southeast Asia 9

tar 10, 11
taxes 5, 25, 37, 38
tobacco companies 6, 25, 34,
   35, 38

U.K. 6, 42, 43
U.S.A. 6, 7, 9, 34, 43

violence 17, 36, **36**

withdrawal symptoms 28
women 7, **7**, 9
World Health Organization 8,
   18, 37

Zambia 6